Wasteland to Eden

Ashley Hoffman

Presentation by *BookLeaf Publishing*

Web: www.bookleafpub.com

E-mail: info@bookleafpub.com

ISBN: 9789357214247

First edition 2023

Dedicated to my children. I pray that the Love of our magnificent Creator finds you wherever you are on your journey. And I pray that you would pursue what He has for you over what the world places at your feet. You won't regret it.

ACKNOWLEDGEMENT

I couldn't have written this book without my wonderful husband, whom has always encouraged me lovingly, provided for me graciously, and given me the freedom to simply bloom.

PREFACE

This book came into being by a lifetime of wrong thoughts, decisions and actions. This resulted in a cloud of darkness encompassing me like a prison. Thoughts of not wanting to be a part of this world anymore made their way into the midst of my mind.

In the deep depths of these thoughts, Jesus graciously met with me. I knew of Him, by what the world told me, but I did not know Him personally. I have come to find out through personal experience that my thoughts on God, based upon the worlds perspective, were entirely and drastically wrong.

I was gifted the words, "Don't do it, God has bigger plans for you," by Him that day. These words made me shake and tremble. The hairs on my arms raised. How could He possibly know what I was thinking?

These words changed the course of my destiny, and I believed right then and there that God was and is absolutely real. I was given the opportunity to start over. I was given a clean slate and a fresh start. I was given so many things that I believed I did not deserve, based on my past. And I stumbled along, even in the midst of a clean slate.

Jesus did not look at my past or my stumbles. He was looking at my future, from His point of view. And so I walked the path from Wasteland to Eden- with Him and His Promises for me. Which have never failed. If you find yourself in a dark place today, and this book reaches your hands, I pray that His Words to me would also speak to you as well. God has bigger plans for you.

Much Grace, Peace, and Love to you, Ashley.

Bench

On a bench I sat.
At the end of my rope.
Drowning in pain.
Alone.
No hope.
I wanted to end it.
My life that day.
An easy exit.
Why should I stay?
A man came.
He stood by me.
He told me He was sent here.
He had a plea.
He knew what I was thinking.
What was going on inside.
He told me not to do it.
That God had bigger plans in mind.
My hands starting shaking.
Who is God?
My hairs started raising.
And my heart throbbed.
I walked away changed.
The tears they fell.
Not due to pain-
Due to knowing full well.

I was just saved.
From the grips of hell.

Love Wins

Walking on eggshells.
Afraid to stand.
Afraid to say.
Gun waving around.
Don't smile.
Obey.
No family.
No friends.
Isolate.
Take your keys away.
No escape.
The Word of Life.
Gathering dust each day.
Pick it up.
Read.
And secretly pray.
A shelter of safety.
Brings a new day.
A voice of hope.
A light ray.
Strength arose.
The screams fade.
Fear doesn't stay.
Love wins this game.

Prophecy

You looked past my shame.
You looked past my chains.
You looked right through my sin.
You looked right through my pain.
And you spoke into me.
Right through the deep.
You spoke Love.
Like I'd never seen.
Words that free.
Prophecy.

Void Inside

There was a void inside.
I tried to fill.
With sex and drugs.
And the cheapest thrills.

There was a void inside.
That I wanted hide.
A pain I masked.
From the world outside.

There was a void inside.
That ached and pained.
I bandaged it up with bars and booze.
It always bled through.

There was a void inside.
And I didn't know why.
It's been there all the while.
Since I was a little child.

There was a void inside.
That rushed me through.
Another day gone.
Another day blue.

There was a void inside.
That crushed my dreams.
Filled me with fear.
And deep anxiety.

There was a void inside.
That made me want to scream.
I was weeping-
And gnashing my teeth.

There was a void inside.
That told me lies.
It fed me the world-
And expected me to smile.

The void inside.
Was missing you.
Jesus-
Gave me His heart.
And made me new.

You filled the void.
You turned off the noise.
You brought Peace.
Love and Joy.

Heard my Cries

I was lost in a pit of all my mistakes.
I was bound and determined to stay chained to
my pain.
And you heard my cries.
Your Love gave me Life.
I was crying out.
God where are you?
Please help me now.
Please see me through.
And you heard my cries.
You opened my eyes.
This world had my convinced they were just
words in a book.
I had to see for myself. I had to take a look.
You told me to set down my burdens.
You told me to set down my hurting.
So I set it down at the foot of the cross.
I called your name and said, 'take it all.'
And I cried out.
God, show me The Way.
Where is this narrow path?
I don't want to stay.
He said- It's not just a book, just some words on
a page.
It's the Word of Life, and I came to Save.

Your Love broke my chains.
Freed me from my pain.
I can't help but exclaim your name.

Dug Up The Gold

This world covered me in dirt.
Poured on the hurt.
Took aim at my heart.
With words that were dark.
Tore my soul right apart.
My God, He dug up the gold.
Gave meaning to this life, something to hold.
His promises never break. His Love never fades.
I needed a place to hide.
A place to run.
From this world.
And the darkness it pours on.
A home to rest.
A place to go.
A life worth living.
Love for my soul.
I needed a place to be seen.
A shelter of Grace.
That I could go to.
No matter the size of my mistake.
You washed me.
And made a new way.
I needed a place of peace.
To find who I was created to be.
The Cross made a way for me.

My Saviors Love.
Set me free.
This world covered me in dirt.
Poured on the hurt.
Took aim at my heart.
With words that were dark.
Tore my soul right apart.
My God, He dug up the gold.
Gave meaning to this life, something to hold.
His promises never break. His Love never fades.

Sinners

I'm so glad He has the Love to see, past our sin into what could be.
He hung out with sinners like me.
His Grace freed, what condemnation bound to me.
He hung out with sinners like me.
If not for your Grace, where would I be?
He hung out with sinners like me.
I'd be stuck in my sin, stuck in my past.
Stuck in the place, that you came to erase.
He hung out with sinners like me.
It is no longer a conspiracy, Christ came to set the captives free.
He hung out with sinners like me.
By Grace, through faith, is The Way, He Saves.
He hung out with sinners like me.

Sting

If I told you all the things I've done.
You wouldn't believe, that I am loved.
My God pulled me from the grave.
Took my sin and took my shame.
Led me to victory.
Broke my chains.
So I'll praise His name.
With all the breath, that I have in my lungs.
I'll sing to you.
For where I am, is better than where I'm from.
You are the beginning of Life, and the end of death.
The sting of sin, led me to your breath.

Faith

I can't see.
It's so dark.
Are you even real?
Do you hear my heart?
-
I am making a way.
For you.
I will finish what I started.
It's true.
I said it.
I will do it.
You'll see.
In the meantime.
Praise me.
Signed,
The King of Kings.

Easy Yoke

I'm going a little crazy.
A little out of my mind.
You said your yoke was easy.
You said your burden was light.
It's feeling a little heavy.
Like I don't have the might.
So I walked away from the system.
The legalism.
Was too tight.
And I sought after your Kingdom.
The Way.
The Truth.
The Life.
And you ripped off my burdens.
Replaced my blindness with sight.
You paid for my sins.
And exchanged the war on my mind.
With Love, Grace and Truth.
You gave me your strength. Your might.
To do what I could never do.
On my own, without you.
Jesus,
Thank you.

Wish Upon A Flower

When the journey gets tough.
And you are feeling alone.
Like nobody knows.
What you are feeling inside.
A deep pain.
That hides.
-

You don't need to wish upon a flower.
He's here, this very hour.
-

Like a breeze that blows through.
His spirit it moves.
Looking for hearts.
That long for the Truth.
Ones like yours.
With a deep ache for more.
-

You don't need to wish upon a flower
He's here, this very hour.
-

Like it's an uphill climb.
A battle that won't subside.
A longing to be free.
And you just can't seem to fly.
On the verge of a breakdown.

Keep trying and trying.
And nothing is happening.
All I'm doing is crying.
-

You don't need to wish upon a flower.
He's here, this very hour.
-

Like a breeze that blows through.
His Spirit it moves.
Looking for hearts.
That long for the Truth.
Ones like yours.
With a deep ache for more.
-

You don't need to wish upon a flower
He's here, this very hour.

Rest in You

The Old Testament me.
Tried to earn His Love.
Laws and rules.
I give up.
The New Testament is HE.
Died to give me Life.
Died to set me free.
All I have to do.
Is rest in you.
-
Drop your weapons.
Drop your swords.
I AM the God.
That wins the war.
Be still and know.
Rest in me.
Surrender all-
Your anxiety.

Grace Path

When His Grace finds you.
When you've been made new.
Things can feel a little confused.
Mountain tops and valleys low.
Where am I now?
Where am I to go?
Jesus and Grace leads you home.
All you've known all this time.
Is a life where you've barely survived.
Lost in a world of fast paced time.
And He sets you on this path basically blind.
Close your eyes from what you see.
Follow me into the deep.
A place reserved for you and me.
A land that flows with milk and honey.
Leave the things you once knew.
They are now behind you.
Look up to what He has.
Can't you perceive it?
Different plans.
A Life with more than you can dream of.
Abundant Love, seated above.
Letting go of things once known.
Blindly walking into the unknown.
It takes a step of faith.

Going in.
Seeking His face.
You don't need to be afraid.
Where you are going.
Is better than where you came.
Set down your chains.
Set down your shame.
You are free.
You have a new name.
You don't need to play Satan's games.
Renew your mind.
Let Grace rain.

Wherever I Am

There's a place I go, where I am free.
To soak up your love for me.
And I'm not sure why.
After all I've done.
How it is even possible.
To be worthy of your love.
There's a place I go, where I am free.
To soak up your love for me.
At first I thought I had to earn my way.
And I tried so hard, everyday.
To find your love. To find my place.
There's a place I go, where I am free.
To soak up your love for me.
I had to stomp on my religion.
Make a way for Grace upon Grace.
You counted my tears, but not my mistakes.
There's a place I go, where I am free.
To soak up your love for me.
And that place I go, is wherever I am.
Because, wherever I am, you are there with me.

Darkness

Darkness tries to rub in my face.
My past.
My sins.
My worst mistakes.
Darkness tries to rule my mind.
With thoughts and lies.
It attempts to bind.
Darkness tries to cover Grace.
With rules and laws.
Trying to get me to earn my place.
But it does not stand
It runs and flees.
When the light of Christ.
Dawns upon me.
God, He sees me as I am.
Here and now.
In Christ.
No longer in Adam.
Darkness is a defeated foe.
A lying enemy.
That lost its supremacy.
For Christ is now my identity.

All Along

I fought so hard.
I tried to fight.
All my wars.
Going on inside.
My strength failed.
Each time I tried.
I can't do this.
In my own might.
I kept stumbling.
Falling.
Trying.
I felt the sting of dying.
I chose the world and not your feet.
I was a Martha and not a Mary.
Your Grace chased me down.
Fought for me.
Brought me back to your feet.
All along you were there.
When I couldn't see.
When I couldn't hear.
I fought you the whole way.
You never gave up.
You never caved.
You've never left my side.
Not a moment in time.

Looking back, I see you.
Molding me.
Carrying me through.
How could I not praise you?

Home

Keep me in step with you wherever I go.
Jesus, you are my home.
As I walk with you.
Take me to all the places that glorify you.
This life is yours to do what only you can do.
Where I walk, I trust you, to bring me through.
Into the dark, the deepest parts, I'll go with you.
There is nowhere else I'd rather be.
Life with you, is home to me.
Keep me in step with you wherever I go.
Jesus, you are my home.
If I dare run ahead of you, make me fall.
Do what you have to do, to get me back to you.
I've seen life that is not quite what it seems.
If you are not there, nor do I, want to be.
I've tasted death and I've tasted Life.
If the choice is mine, I don't want anything,
except you by my side.
Keep me in step with you wherever I go.
Jesus, you are my home.

Gift

I hold out my gift when you least deserve a reach.
I hold out my gift as you walk off and stray.
Trying to make your own way.
But I whisper.
I'm here to stay.
I hold out my gift.
When you refuse my Love.
When you run from my Grace.
But I will touch your heart with my embrace.
I hold out my gift.
As you cause me heart break.
When you hurt the very people.
I want you to Love.
But I whisper.
You are forgiven.
The gift I've given.
Is enough.
I hold out my gift.
As you sob and grieve.
Over My Love for you.
And the time it took for you to believe.
I hold out my gift.
And whisper.
I understand.

It takes time to change minds.
But my patience waits until Love arrives.
I holds out my gift.
And whisper.
It's free.
For people like you.
To be.
Wrapped in my Love.
Eternally.
The gift of me.
-Jesus

Umbrella

Standing under an umbrella.
Of self condemnation.
Shame.
Repeated mistakes.
Seems there is no escape.
Gunk and junk have taken claim.
Put down the umbrella.
It is a religious façade.
Keeping you in it's mist.
Blocking your Grace.
It has all been conquered.
Buried in the grave.
You are freed and forgiven.
Believe in His name.
Jesus, He made a way.
The bondage is broken.
The Kingdom awaits.
Put down the umbrella.
And let Grace REIGN.

Keep Walking

I know you've cried out a hundred times.
All the tears that have fell from your eyes.
Feeling alone like there's no end in sight.
Walking along and there's no finish line.
He wants you to know that He's by your side.
Walking with you every step, every stride.
Jesus He came, He gave up his life.
For every soul, every sin, far and wide.
He conquered the grave, death and night.
He's with you now, so don't give up this fight.
Rest in His promises.
Keep walking.
And you'll see-
The light.

ChristMAS.

Christmas means more- Of Christ.
Hallelujah! A son is born- Tonight.

Christmas is for- everyday, evermore.
Eternal Life. Glory to the Lord.

In a manger He laid.
It was my debts He paid.
I put Him on the cross that day.
Ashamed of what I'd done.
I wanted to look away.
His blood was the only way.

A gift to the world.
Free of charge.
A Savior born.
In our hearts.

What better gift could we receive.
My sin washed. My life redeemed.
All because of what you did for me.
On the cross, the day you died for me.

Christmas means more- Of Christ.
Hallelujah! A son is born- Tonight.

Christmas is for- everyday, evermore.
Eternal Life. Glory to the Lord.

A gift to the world.
The Father gave.
A double edged sword.
He came to save.
Revelation Word.
Cut like a knife.
Right to my heart.
The Word of Life.
Sometimes I wonder what I did.
To receive such a Love.
It's nothing I did.
That's why it's a gift.
A gift to the world.
A Savior.
A Son.
His Kingdom come.
Hallelujah!
Merry Christmas, everyone!

Christmas means more- Of Christ.
Hallelujah! A son is born- Tonight.

Christmas is for- everyday, evermore.
Eternal Life. Glory to the Lord.